Animals
Keeping Safe

Jane Burton

Random House 🏠 New York

First American Edition, 1989

Text and photographs copyright © 1989 by Jane Burton. Compilation copyright © 1989 by Belitha Press. All rights reserved under International and Pan-American Copyright Conventions. Published in the United States by Random House, Inc., New York. Originally published in Great Britain by Belitha Press Ltd., London, in 1989.

Library of Congress Cataloging-in-Publication Data: Burton, Jane.
Animals keeping safe. SUMMARY: Photographs and text depict how animals use teeth, claws, spikes, horns, camouflage, poison, and other ways to protect themselves from their enemies. 1. Animal defenses— Juvenile literature. 2. Animal weapons—Juvenile literature. [1. Animal defenses. 2. Animal weapons] I. Title. QL759.B87 1989 591.57 88-43152 ISBN: 0-394-82263-3 (pbk.); 0-394-92263-8 (lib. bdg.)

Manufactured in Hong Kong 1 2 3 4 5 6 7 8 9 0

◀ Animals are always on the alert. The gray squirrel keeps watch the whole time he is eating. High in a tree, he is safe from enemies on the ground—but he must watch out for dangerous birds flying overhead.

Cautious house mice feeding in a group take turns being the lookout. ▲

The water hole is a dangerous place. A lioness may be lurking in the bushes nearby, knowing that thirsty animals *must* come to drink—there is no other water for miles around. Animals never come to a water hole alone if they can help it. They always come in herds. The more eyes, ears, and noses there are to detect danger, the safer the animals will be.

While the zebras put their heads down to drink, the giraffes keep watch. If something startles the giraffes, the zebras will be frightened, too, and run to safety.

◀ Pearl can protect herself by running away, or she can lash out with her sharp claws and teeth. But her ten-day-old kitten, Benjamin, is too little to protect himself. Pearl looks after him and keeps him safe. She is purring now, but she will turn into a spitting, slashing fury if anyone tries to hurt Benjamin.

▼ Honey is sweet and gentle with her puppies. She licks Gem's face and cuddles Fan. Her pups are just eleven days old and very helpless; they can crawl but cannot see and have no teeth. If they are threatened, Honey will leap to defend them, snarling and biting if necessary.

▲ Many animals keep their babies safe in a warm nest while they are little and helpless. This Egyptian gerbil is gathering dry grass to make a nest in an underground burrow. If she senses danger, she will carry her babies one by one to a safer place.

Baby moorhens are born on top of a big mound of reeds. The first chicks stay in the nest until all the eggs have hatched. Then they splash into the water and swim after their parents, who watch over them and warn them when danger is near. ▶

Usually it is the mother fish who looks after the eggs, but sometimes the father is the baby-sitter. The male worm pipefish is hard to find among the brown seaweed. He carries his eggs safely stuck to his belly. ▲

▼ In a fast-flowing stream, the male bullhead guards his eggs near a large stone.

The female African mouthbreeder carries her eggs in her mouth to keep them safe. When the babies hatch, she lets them out to swim and feed. If a big fish swims by, the babies rush back to her mouth. She gobbles them up, then carries them away to a safer place. There she spits them all out again, being very careful not to swallow any.

◀ Some animals have homes they can dash to for safety. Others carry their homes with them. The soft bodies of garden snails are covered with slime to keep them wet. Since snails need to stay wet all the time, they only come out of their shells at night or when it rains. During hot weather they go back into their shells to avoid the sun.

▲ The shell of the painted topshell is very strong. If this snail sees a big fish coming, it quickly clamps down and shuts itself tightly into its shell.

The red-eared terrapin can tuck its head, legs, and tail right inside its shell when danger threatens. Or it can plop into the water and swim away to safety. ▲

All sorts of soft-bodied animals take over other animals' shells after the owners have finished with them.

▲ The hermit crab's legs and claws are tough, but its body is very soft, and coiled to fit inside a snail shell. When danger looms, the hermit retreats right inside its shell, closing the entrance with a claw. As the hermit grows up, it gets too big for its shell and looks for a larger one. It feels around inside the new shell with its claws to make sure it is empty, then quickly walks out of its tight old shell and into the bigger new one.

A common octopus has caught a crab. The octopus curls up safely inside a large triton shell to enjoy its meal. ▲

▲ Fishes take refuge in any nooks and crannies they can find, so empty shells make good hiding places.

Blennies live in rock pools on the seashore. The smaller one has been hiding in the castoff shell of a shore crab. The crab who left this empty shell did not die, it just changed its skin. A crab's skin is hard and rigid and does not grow with the crab like a snail's shell grows with the snail. The crab makes a soft new skin inside the old one. The dead skin cracks and the crab backs out.

A swan mussel used to live inside this hinged shell, but it died. Something ate away its soft body. Now a pair of mouthbreeders take shelter in its shell. ▲

An arrow-poison frog does not need to hide. Frog-eating animals leave it alone because its bright color warns them that it is poisonous. South American Indians put its poison on their arrowheads. The poison is so strong that if an arrow tipped with it just grazes the skin, the victim will die.

Horns over its eyes and on its snout make the horned-nose frog look fierce. No smaller animal is safe from this frog because anything that crawls near is snapped up into its wide mouth. The frog keeps *itself* from being eaten by looking so much like a dead leaf that it is invisible as long as it stays still!

Nasty insects are often brightly colored. Some that are black with red spots are *very* nasty.

▼ The red blister beetle sits on a leaf in the bright sunshine. When picked up, it oozes a poisonous fluid that burns the skin and makes painful blisters.

Most moths are brown and fly at night. Birds and bats like to eat them. The brightly colored six-spot burnet moth buzzes around when the sun is shining. It sits on flowers and is easy for birds to see. But if a bird pecks one, yellow drops of acid ooze from the moth's neck. One taste, and that bird will never touch another black and red insect again!　　　　　▼

Most wasps and hornets are black-and-yellow striped. They are safe from attack because their stripes advertise that they sting. Everyone fears a wasp sting.

▼ The wasp beetle has no sting, but it is striped like a wasp and moves in a jerky, wasp-like way. Birds leave it alone.

The harmless ant beetle also pretends to be a wasp. It looks like a kind of wasp called a velvet ant, which is black and white and has a very bad sting. ▼

Both of these beetles are harmless and stay safe because they pretend to be harmful wasps.

▲ A bull's-eye moth is hard to see when it rests on a tree with its wings closed. If something disturbs it, the moth flicks open its wings, suddenly flashing the bright eyespots on its underwings. The eyespots look like the eyes of a large and menacing animal—perhaps a saw-whet owl, a dangerous bird of prey. ▶

▼ Hedgehogs are very prickly and have strong, sharp spines instead of soft fur on their backs. When startled, the first thing a hedgehog does is put its head down and its prickles up. If a fox or a dog tries to sniff it, the hedgehog "huffs" and jerks. It pricks the predator on the nose! The wounded animal yelps and usually leaves the hedgehog alone. But if a really hungry fox still tries to bite it, the hedgehog quickly rolls up into a tight ball. Curled up like that, with prickles sticking out in all directions, a hedgehog is completely safe.
▼

▼ Sea urchins are round and covered with sharp spines, like a curled-up hedgehog. The hatpin urchin has very long spines. They are not only as sharp as needles, they are poisonous as well. If the hatpin urchin feels something with the tip of one spine, it points lots of other spines in the same direction.

The diadem urchin waves its spines as it travels across the rocks. It walks on some of the short, stubby spines; the longer spines are weapons that keep the urchin safe. ▼

White rhinoceroses are huge beasts. They wallow in mud or dust. They bother nobody as long as nobody bothers them. But if angry, they charge like tanks and trample and gore their enemy. Because of their size and strength and bad temper, all other animals leave rhinos alone.

But rhinos have enemies more dangerous than any four-legged animal—humans. Poachers kill rhinos whenever they can because rhino horns are worth a lot of money. Game wardens try to guard rhinos and keep them safe in special parks.